Out of Town

Lex Runciman

Northwest Poetry Series

Out of Town

Lex Runciman

First Edition

Library of Congress Cataloging in Publication Data

Lex Runciman, 1951 –
Out of Town

ISBN: 0-9665018-5-3

Cloudbank Books
P.O. Box 610
Corvallis, OR 97339-0610
Cloudbank Books is an imprint of
Bedbug Press, P.O. Box 39, Brownsville, OR 97327

The cover art is a collage by Terry Garrett.
Cover design and book design by M'Liss Runyon.
Cloudbank Books logo is a carving by Julie Hagan Bloch from
Haunting Us With His Love by David Samuel Bloch.
Text set in Bookman. Title type: Sloppy Ink and Skia
Printed in Canada by Friesens, Altona, Manitoba

This book is for three women.

My thanks to the editors of the following magazines in which many of these poems (sometimes in earlier forms) first appeared:

Caffeine Destiny
College English
Fireweed
Hubbub
ISLE
Jefferson Monthly
Meridian
Missouri Review
Nebraska Review
New England Review
Northwest Review
Open Spaces
Terrain
Testmarketed Downpour
Poetry East
Quarterly West
Santa Clara Review
Southern Review
Talking River Review
Verse
Willow Springs

"Day Litany" first appeared in *The Oregonian*.

"The Moon" first appeared in *O Poetry, O Poesia: Poems of Oregon and Peru*, edited by Joseph Soldati and Eduardo Gonzales-Viana, published by Western Oregon University.

Thanks to the Oregon Institute of Literary Arts
(now Literary Arts Inc.)
for a grant that enabled me to begin some of these poems.

Special thanks to collaborators and friends Chris Anderson, Lee Bassett, and Paul Cook; to my wise and generous colleagues at Linfield College; to editors Chris Howell, Erik Muller, Lisa Steinman, and Jessie Lendennie; and in particular to Tony Gorsline, Peter Sears, Michael Malan and all the company at Cloudbank Books.

CONTENTS

I.

II.

III.

I.

One Thing

In the garden
Before everything fell into its separateness,
Before everything fell apart,
The mute and noisy world sang—it was one thing—
And we had no need, no need for speech.

Pears and the mayfly hatch were one thing.
And plums withering and olives littering the floor
Were one thing. And what the spiders said spinning,
What slugs intoned, what onions in their harmonies grew,
What a kestrel's eye understood and the mosquitoes knew
And what leeches and eels contemplated in their solitude
Was one thing. The arc of the sun rising and Venus rising
And the moon peering at us with its rheumy eye
And papyrus in the backwash, the kelp forest
And the swoop of bats and their dreamless sleep
And the open mouths of poppies, and sand dunes,
A drift of camas, a cane thicket, jackrabbits,
And purple vetch, a stand of wheat or mustard or daisies,
A horse with its nostrils flared to the wind
Was one thing.

Afterwards, for our consolation and despair,
Our guessing and second guessing, our anger and stammer
And painful joy, we had to learn to speak to learn
How clumsy we had become
And wrong, foolish, arrogant, partial, and loud.
It's all we can do to think the world we breathe in,
The chant and rhythm of it, catching
The unsayable shape and echo
Which was one thing—speech
And silence, certainty and doubt,
The wakefulness and the sleeping,
The error and the remedy.

Motel Flamingo Pool

Santa Rosa, California, 1959. Sunshine
as advertised, sunshine in a Pantone sky
over a chlorine-blue pool, over divers
briefly airborne, over swimmers and bathers
lounging with cigars, over a boy in a canvas chair.

Five days earlier, sometime in the dark,
the endless intensity of his ache stopped.
It woke him and he turned on a light. His room
was his room. His pillow was yellowed, slightly
bloodied, but his ear felt so much better
he felt tired. He slept all night with the light on

until they woke him. And they took him with them anyway
—on vacation. They rode in a Buick for three days
and he threw up once on an old blanket his father
rolled into a ball and lobbed into the Sacramento River.
Now he is forbidden to swim. His brother
drifts in his mother's arms, and his father
sounds and surfaces like a whale.

Wearing a tee shirt and his suit, the boy sits.
He sits in shallow water on the pool's second step.
He sits with a man smoking Havanas
who is paunchy, tattooed, whose mouth talks
around a wet cigar
baseball and the Korean War. Amazing to watch, hard to hear.
He listens, half listens. The drain at the bottom of the pool
distorts and wavers after every dive.
And whenever he leans back, his feet rise

like heavy balloons, and water spills
into the hollow of his navel.
That life is not fair is a bitter lesson.
On an afternoon hotter than Oregon ever is,

he may watch the pool. He may sit on the second step
and lean back. He may talk to a stranger
or walk on the bottom, which everyone knows is
the hardest way to move through water. But he may not
—doctor's orders—he may not go under.

And sooner or later
they will all ask him, Are you having fun?
His father will rise up dripping
and ask him that. His mother
will finish toweling her hair which looks mussed
and ridiculous, and she will ask him.
And then his innocent brother will echo it
as he shakes pool water out of his healthy ears.

Missouri Air

A room. A boy in his bed.
He has opened the window.

A car passes. Wind moves the curtains.
He watches shadows half show what he keeps:
Quartz, shell fossils, gray sheath knife,
A bat hiding failure deep in its grain—
One day at the plate it will shatter.
And magazines, books, Converse shoes,
Underwear, jeans and other junk in that dark
Only a streetlight brightens and the moon.

Almost ready to be easily, fully asleep,
He doesn't care about the day ending.
His legs want to bend a little and do.
His arm wants to shift a little and it does.
He reaches for the sheet's double fabric,
Slides the rounded edge between his fingers,
Thinks of rectangles, halves doubled over
And brighter in the sun than mirrors.
Hanging on a line, sheets can sound like flags,
Like huge blank banners flapping near the bath towels,
Pillow cases, diapers and boxers, bras
And the round-neck shirts. He helps his mother
Gather them into a wide wicker basket.

He knows this.
He knows the details of his life
So thoroughly he doesn't wonder why
All summer the utility room dryer stays quiet,
A surface for sorting or folding
Or for the pairing of socks.
He knows his grandmother

Only as a young woman in an old picture.
It will be decades before he understands
She had no dryer but Missouri air
Which freely she took pleasure in.
As did her daughter, his mother,
Who made a clean texture and a bright smell
Part of his falling asleep in summer.

Drill

When the fire bell rang one long,
Two short, one long, two short, and kept on,
It meant war not fire. It meant Sister Louise Teresa
Must close the hallway doors
And lower rows of Venetian blinds over the 48 windows,
Each row narrowing our city with its river,
With Mt. Tabor and Ross Island and the bridges like
Rigid latticework, like lace behind the maple branches,
Though by then we weren't supposed to be watching her
In her black with white blinders,
The habit hiding her face—
We never saw her afraid.

Facing away from where the flash would come,
We crouched down and wondered if we'd burn.
Pretzeled in the leg-space of our desks, we rested
Our heads on our knees and our hands on our heads,
While the bell kept on, for as long as it rang.
And we were supposed to not think of anything ending,
And we were not to pray for ourselves (a form
Of pride and greed) but could ask God's mercy
On strangers, the Russians in their cities
With watery rivers, their foreign children.

We all sinned. We prayed for hamsters
And parents. I prayed for Mrs. Shea, who was regular—
Not a Sister—and so needed prayers.
I prayed for my brother and everything in my drawer,
For the butt and the feet that tingled—
Parts more venial than praying for the mortal whole.
After awhile the bell was just a rhythm, Mrs. Cook
Humming in her library. So I thought of her,
Who knew my name and was kind to me
And could fit under no desk.

Gore

In that filtered, undemolished room, the light
ivoried, unreal, a bald man swims in his sleep
on a chaise lounge by a box radio bright with tubes,
noisy with static and play-by-play, the re-creations
of away games, crack of the bat and crowd noise,
a double header from Fenway, a whole Saturday.

A woman smokes looking west to drift logs,
tumbled smooth, salt-soaked, dry-rotting home
to squirrels she feeds loaf ends, squirrels I wait for
but never long enough—all that sand, kelp whips and shells.
When the snoring man wakes he watches barges,
shipping news on his lap, binoculars
to miss everything but distance. He watches
and the summer flies, blue bodies and commons,
buzz his popcorn and land weighty on his neck or ear.
I'm hired: dime a fly, bodies in a jelly jar.

When a skate dies, the diamond of its body
washes ashore and rots. Murres too, the occasional
seal carcass like a pillow, razor clams like knives.
I worked afternoons with a swatter flies were smart enough
not to fly at. Hands were the best tools: imagine
a flight path, clap inches over the wings.

The skate has a mouth and sand worms find it first.
It gets larger and loses shape. Worms don't like
light—they go back to sand. Gulls empty the eyes first.
My hands go greasy with abdomens, wings and thorax
I must assemble for the count. I have this memory
peopled with the dead, with glare and windy sunshine,
a beach, a happy boy, flies and dimes.

1958-1968

Slowly we perfected the art of watching:
Out the steamy window the hawthorn dropping its leaves,
Wonder Bread down in the chrome toaster, elements glowing,
Milk poured for us in green glasses, the table set,
Butter, and salt and pepper shakers,
The sliced, paper-thin chipped beef simmering
In a floury gravy, and the television on—

That astonishment of motion, of sound and place,
Washington, D.C., imagine it in your own kitchen,
In every kitchen in the country, the same
Cathode-ray glow, the same person
Whose name everyone knows, a face white
And black and leaning in so frank with the truth,
Someone alive and distant, the technology
Of the impossible become possible.

Once all those hours of labor were spent,
The set had to be on. Sound down or not,
It had to do its job, demonstrate a paycheck,
A cheerful if borrowed faith in American things,
Images as numerous and changeable as promises,
The news from Chicago or Tuscaloosa or New York
National, larger than ours, clearer, more
Concise, at once visible and farther away.

We watched.
We watched drought and catastrophe,
Said grace, pass the pepper, how was your day?
We chewed, swallowed, kept our napkins on our laps,
Watched and ate and watched Wilma Rudolph run
In Rome, our first Olympics, her running free of polio
Like nothing we had ever seen.

So it took more than chipped beef, creamed onions,
Or salmon loaf or tuna casserole, more than College Bowl
Or To Tell the Truth, it took a war to make us stop.
Day after day of dead and wounded,
Even without color you could tell the color.
It took protest marches and body counts.
It took napalm and pacification and people screaming

Over the rotors of helicopter gunships,
Over the staccato of rifle fire—it took weeks of this,
Years, with meat loaf and milk and fresh-picked sweet corn
Before it entirely replaced our conversation. Midmeal
One late summer evening, my mother slid her chair back,
Stood, walked over to the counter and turned it all off—
Just a quiet, gray box. Then she sat down.

She kept on eating, so we did,
Our knives and forks loud on our plates,
The kitchen door open and no one saying anything.

Two Songs by Harry Warren

Roused by strange rhythms from sleep,
      a child frowns in the dark,
climbs from bed and edges down a dim hall.
      Around the corner, the living room
is day-bright, dark at the windows, that music
      —Krupa, Sinatra, Etta James—
like water they're swimming in.
      Slicked back, the man's dark hair
gleams. The woman holding his hand out
      is dancing, shoes off, hair swaying.
Her hips limber and shoulders in a rhythm
      as she moves, smiling, eyes closed.
He's looking at her.

Night like you've never waked in,
      all light and music. Five years old
and you'll be scolded sure—or invisible,
      whichever's worse. They see you.
Your mother sweeps you up and you all three
      sway, a slower motion.
Tall and between them, warm,
      slumped as a sack of flour.
You close your eyes.
      In this dream music making time,
No one speaks. And no one now to say—
      not confirm nor revise nor contradict.
Lullaby of Broadway. At Last.

Young at Heart

It's nothing like home, how television fills a room
—The fashionable hour when Rosalind
Floor-length-silk Russell saunters in.
The maitre d' bows. And every table is smooth linen,
Crystal and silver for two—no children—
And every patron extra smokes.

When he joins her, Fred MacMurray doesn't notice
How she leans in on both elbows, an old fashioned
And a cigarette In the same lustrous hand. Poor Fred.
He stares past that gorgeous face and says,
"A man can make something of himself in Chicago."
Chin down, half not-smiling, she looks at him.

He inhales, the Chesterfield glows white,
He closes the lighter with a metallic click, sighs, sits back.
Her silence cues the orchestra: A slow, lush number
Both of them know. Supper never arrives.
They dance. They hold each other
Not timidly exactly, but as though the female body

And the male body would both always be offering
And mystery and mobile grace on the dance floor.
They have practiced this all their lives, this dancing
As though they are almost sleeping, as though
They know music and liquor will take them somewhere.
And for as long as they dance, she believes
She believes she loves him. And he loves the shiny floor,

Loves her hair, loves his shoes and the drape of his suit
And the feel of her back, cash in his pocket like music—
He loves himself dancing with her.

Like Men

Though I knew them in homes and work,
In argument and quiet, and loved them,
They were inarticulate and they liked to hit.
Born to absorb punishment like men,
Born to dish it out—even as little boys
They were sex-driven, the losers and the winners.
For five or six generations (which was longer
Than they could remember), they worked hard
To become cogs, gears, the grease or the machine
At salary, hourly, or piece rates.
If lucky, they bullied others; if not, they went surly
And in their perversity never missed a day.
They spent long hours learning numb,
Learning repetition, learning boredom.
They were befuddled by the idea of beauty
Until they saw it, until they were seized by it,
Weak-kneed by it, mute and sheepish
And then probably angry. They used women,
Children, dogs as they were used, and the nameless
Remorse they felt drove them to rage, to drink
Or bowl or shoot birds they loved to see flying.
They could be smart about any number of constructions
Including faucets and all the ball sports but tennis.
They could even know what they wanted for others,
What they worked and worked for, though emotion
Embarrassed them: they sent cards
Or bought freezers as surprises.
The paycheck—never enough—was proof
Of love, that word they could not quite
Get in their mouths. They saved
For education for their children, who
If successful, they did not understand, who
Thinking of them, wished them ease
And thanksgiving, and thought pity.

Glass

Out the office window, sidewalk cherries begin to be
ornamental, afternoon winding down, and the phone
rings—Charles Neville, a stranger who remembers my
father a nine-year-old boy, if I can imagine that.

They played, he says, played in a peach orchard with an
old house smack in the middle of it, long lines of trunks
with heavy canopies, then a saggy porch fronting grimed,
wavy windows—two casements flanking the nailed door,
one more on the west wall, two on the east. Late afternoon,
he says, one day they broke every window, stoned them all
for the pure thrill of breaking something fragile. For the
sound it made again and again, the sound of glass. "We
loved it," he says, all pleasure in memory, "that wild
craziness souring only at the end. Then we went home."

My father says Charlie always tells that story. And lately
I've been picturing blossoms drifted on a porch like snow,
pear blossoms since I know those trees. I've been picturing
that house, dark settled in the cupped steps, a thin,
widening line of twilight rising between the chimney and
the wall. We've been here before. We've piled up river rocks
and just carrying one around I've warmed it. Sky going
dark, I stand sideways and look over my shoulder at
Charlie who's standing sideways. We see each other. I
wind up, figuring we're pretending like always, and I'm not
thinking about anything but how weight shifts and
shoulders turn.

I can feel the heft and surface and curve of that washed
stone, then it's out of my hand. It's out of my hand, rising
a little, side-slipping flat away, and it's beautiful even
though I know where it's going and what will happen—the
guilt and the whipping. It sails on the air, spinning.

When That Was

before the swingset
rocked with our weight (my own and Bruce's)
like a chair on an uneven floor

before lawn bordered by daffodils
not lawn but lettuce butter lettuce
romaine Brussels sprouts slick dimpled peppers
celery sweet carrots like fingers
red onions radishes bush beans

my father's garden
my father on his knees weeding with a trowel
standing with a soaker he directs to the roots of his crop
summer dusk and dark enough
we see his cigarette whenever he inhales
he's thinking about something besides bedtime
because he lets us wander past the bird bath
under shore pines where stars disappear

before reading or grief
before sickness occurred to us
the year my brother almost two let go the redwood bench
and walked right off the concrete onto the grass
no one else there no one else
to see him topple forward and not fall
and not fall and
not fall

Lila Singing

Amazing Grace, voice pure as a girl's.
Not Agatha, tubercular and dead at fourteen,
Not Judy Garland: Lila next door, Lila singing.
So Maude Peterson knows where she is.

Where we are, it's late, kids asleep.
I'm dozing, their mother showering, wind
Down East Canyon humming over the chimney like a bottle.
The phone jolts me upright—an old woman's voice
Saying my own, my oldest name,
Though I am not nine.

Franciscan china, a rock maple table and chairs—
All we speak of reappears: the glassy porch
With her beach shoes and grandpa's,
Sand dollars, limpets, turbans on the sills.
She talks about her Hollywood house.
I remember a window taller than I am,
Blue sky and green trees waving—
An oriental carpet the day I learned to walk.

After illness and so many years,
I want this conversation,
I want this astonishment and calm return
To last, but it doesn't. I have to understand
She has other calls. I say
How good it has been to talk with her.
Yes, she says.

Funeral Home Attendant

Dead weight. God's pesto. Heavy jello.
The pitch, roll, and yaw of the chemical.
Bag o'bourbon, sack o'soup.
Branch wood, kindling, in thick socks.
Tucks and pouches full of plumbs.
Thick sleeve of pennies.

Soft lips, forgive us.
Genome undone, forgive us.
Duffel of pianos,
purse, pocket, pillow, wallet,
occlusions and severings,
forgive us our levity.

Everything about it was odd.
A covered porch, hospital vans,
the driver and I wheeling the gurney,
always a bent wheel
like a shopping cart spasming,
shimmying down the aisle.

The living were irrational, susceptible,
required what they required:
show me the ankle scar, please, no more.
Or this arrangement, the particular flower.
One rule, usually easy: give good manners,
a gentleness from strangers.

The best week: five sunny, humid days
without a single child—Wednesday,
Thursday, Friday, Saturday, Sunday.

Adoption

Eating okay, loving toys and loving pets,
we grew up fine. And imagining other parents—
drunk, destitute, living on Ritz crackers
in a '48 Chevy with a corroding tailpipe:
he's unshaven, sullen; and her hair looks this
one way, not attractive; or, strangers still,
they're rich rich—all that was imagination, play.

Dependable, familiar, the real set lived downstairs,
standing at the kitchen counter rifling mail,
pouring drinks, or cooking once the fan when on,
or reading the evening paper, the *Oregon Journal.*
Politics, weather, gossip, business, us—
mostly they talked to each other, the television
and their natural voices mumbling through the floor.

We did grow up fine. School was fine.
We wore pointy hats and gathered around sugary cakes.
In blurry pictures of white candles lit, our cheeks
puff out like blowfish and the flames lean away.
Middle class, mid-century, American. We got more
than our share: outgrown coats older cousins sent,
Schwinns with fat tires, a dog, a turtle, a cat.

Long evenings after dinner, the Big Dipper poured.
We grew up fine. And the play has become habit—
At an airport, say, or walking downtown: she
is your sister. Or her. Or her. He's your second
brother. No, not him, him. Even if we are all
going somewhere else, not exactly homeless,
and usually in a hurry.

Common Story

Now what was done can be said:
His jaw sawed open at his chin, bone
    With half his bottom teeth hinged out,
Nerves for hearing in that ear cut,
    Pulled aside, clamped. This took

An hour, a saw whining, inevitable liquids
    Suctioned, blotted away, until the structure
Encased in tumor, the brain stem, shone.

    X-ray, CAT scan, a representation
Is never the thing. I don't know its color
    Or how it pulsed as everything interior must.
I don't know if just looking you could say
    What was tumor, what was necessary.

I don't know how many people
    Considered this problem their problem,
Much less how Monday, Tuesday, Wednesday, this

    Might be done for strangers again, again—
A whole career of dubious action. I know
    The end is a relentless, slow pursuit
Of the beginning: they finish in reverse,
    Aligning, splicing, reattaching, all the while

This anatomy of motion, my brother—his breathing
    More regular than any natural sleep.
When he wakes, tubes are the entrances and exits.

    He will not swallow for a year. He learns
New contours, schooling muscles for how to speak.
    It works. Scars smooth, and what would
Strangle him or tell his heart stop
    Was itself stopped, catastrophe

So narrowly turned away it's funny.
        Twenty years ago this happened,
Eighty seasons of impossible equations,

        How a calendar, an uncertain future,
Keeps becoming the narrative past.
        We think of it. We think of it
And shake our heads.

Pacific Water, Coastal Air

      We slept, woke to fog,
not ground level and sieving through trees,
      just that color, absence of color—
early television, portraits by Matthew Brady—
      all black and white, water and air,
water as it goes to distance which is gray.

Midmorning.
      Wind a calm breathing,
water sucked into some huge bladder offshore
      for the moon's slow release.
Something faint and infrequent,
      a line of pelicans,
dips and arcs into wave troughs.
      Something uncolored and everywhere,
like delicacy, touches my face, speckles this paper.
      It gathers at the fibrous tips of gulls' wings—
the same color as they go, as they beat twice a second,
      glide and down, glide and down,
and breathing tastes like salt.

Saying Grace

Eleventh month, slant light,
sky cloudless almost, white fuzz at the line horizon makes,
humped hills and the patchy meadows browned,
uncut trees in the distance like a brush swept up
half an inch on laid paper, a watercolor in the foyer.

My mother would think we're doing it wrong,
opening the curtains like this, flooding the room,
fading the carpet and the sofa back.
She'd want to say something but wouldn't
and a timer would buzz or phone or doorbell ring,
and that would be the end of it.
She would close the curtains only after dark,
after pumpkin pie, the creamed onions
saved in their bowl for tomorrow.

Thus where we are recedes before what we remember,
conversations in another room: we are all so happy
to talk again, we have not seen each other in years.
Cardamom and sage, the yeast of baking.
Roast and starch, the simple and vegetable sugars.
Rooms and rooms, all we have and have forgotten,
the dead alive and the living, visits and words
and good drink, warmth in hand—whatever
we have endured, we give thanks for.

II.

November Again

A sleepy child
awakens enough to climb stairs
walk familiar halls dim at this hour
and find our room find us
clock radio on lamp on
covers warm last dreams floating around
and when the child climbs in wordlessly
we slide over wordlessly knowing
we'll all have to rise soon enough

Odd to remember being the child
with oversized flannel pajama bottoms
that I walked on and half tripped over
pulling the covers open
to climb up onto a huge bed
and stretch into the warm shadow
of someone in the shower
someone dressing for work

Happy

"The sky's dream is enormous."
                Robert Penn Warren

Those first awkward weeks,
          seven, eight pounds,
dry, fed, held, rocked, cooed at and sung to,
          you cried. We played Bolero, we danced,
that volume, wail and percussion
          either soothing or terrifying you quiet.
Neighbors' houses darkened. Your eyes closed,
          delicately we'd maneuver you down
to the padded crib. And as your head touched,
          or as we arranged a blanket or turned away,
you would twitch awake, lift your knees under you
          and holler, night after night. At last, tired,
desperate, emptied of anger or intelligence,
          we'd pillow and strap you into the backpack
and walk. It was summer—the nights were warm.
          One of us slept and one of us walked.
We slalomed Higgins, zig and zag, past Evans,
          down Beverly, down South,
pacing yellow stripes one block after another.
          Sometime towards four, even the dark blurs,
concrete and parked houses and motionless cars,
          your posture and the rhythm of your breath
saying I am tired now; truly, I am finally happy.

Whatever Day This Is

On and off shadows
under the residential trees so that
as I drive I squint on and off
as you hold the baby
snoring lightly on your shoulder.

Resting like that,
our daughter looks blissful, relaxed.
She's not. She's exhausted. Whatever
day this is, we've not slept since Tuesday.
We've talked to doctors.
We're following directions to a hospital,
the road seems weirdly mobile,
and you're sitting like sculpture—upright, controlled.

Like money or justice, illness is random.
So doctors describe to us the entire surgical procedure
for a spinal tap on an infant.
Even the surgeon herself looks tired,
or bored, as she angles the pencil
just where on the wall chart the length of needle
must ease in and sidle by the dime-size
saucers of vertebrae which must not move.

The room slows, and whatever day this is,
we nod. They know we're tired,
but they want us to hear the symptoms
of cerebrospinal meningitis, and its complications,
and their seriousness—terrifying and religious.

Whatever day this is, we're counting intersections,
seeing beautiful trees, dogwoods, whites and pinks,
and droopy Himalayan cedars, mown lawns,
all this human landscape
At a light, we stop. I squint.

You look straight ahead. I love you
now and always, whatever day this is, now
and always. I don't remember road or traffic.
I remember like a snapshot
the rosy fold and gentle curve
of a small girl's ear.

The meningitis was a lesser thing.
We slept and slept.

Applause

For preschoolers, the naturally naked,
all clothing is costume, every room a stage,
simple breathing an occasion for charming adults.
But choreographed under ceilingless lights,
music and silence surrounding them,
and faced with the formal regard of relatives
and strangers, children lack discipline:
they grin, they wave. Two of them belong to us.

At intermission, the youngest wood nymphs
return, walking carefully, still costumed, garish,
not quite fresh, shoeless and easy with family
who hug and praise them. Some, too sleepy to stay,
leave as the house lights dim and the music
assumes a new intricacy. Some settle in
to watch the height, glamour and toe shoes they desire.

Hours at the *barre*, hours before the mirror.
In leotards on rainy Tuesdays and Fridays for months
they have stretched, giggled, learned their own silliness
and grace—how each of us bends, flexes, stumbles,
turns and leaps inside a body. They have learned
pliés and *relevés*, the odd spellings of composers'
and each others' names.

Friday night, 10 o'clock.
The auditorium is suffused with hair spray, perfume,
and sweat. Our programs are folded or rolled into tubes.
The still-present company assembles.
As it has all evening, the curtain lifts
like something outside gravity. And we cannot help it.
Some days at home all we say is no and no and no and no.
Now we want to say yes.

No Pictures

No portraits. No wild iris—
white and mottled tongues. No
blue camas, and none of us

after supper past the dead end of our street
where off-road vehicle ruts clog with grasses,
low clover, weeds, where

something on not tall stems crowns
deeply and beguilingly purple, multiple
and purple, like something beautifully sweet.

The dog has raised his leg
and moved on down the trail he smells
Jane has taken, though he cannot see her.

She is seven, lanky, and the wild grains
shimmer higher than her hair.
She's burrowing, walking a tunnel

with edges that every once in awhile kiss
her cheeks. She uses those words.
One book Beth reads says "savanna:

uplands, south facing, often burned by Indians
for berries" (berries we have found
swollen the size of thumbs).

But daisies stopped us that evening—acres of wild
surface above surface, one undulant,
one solid, one praising the other.

None of that either. No Easter, no ballet.
No birthday. No family gathered at Grandma Berry's
ailing fence. "Sorry," the clerk looks at them,

not at me, "no pictures at all—bad film."
Silence. They look at each other. "Oh."
"Oh well. We don't care."

They run ahead, across the asphalt.
They open a car door, stop, look back.
They're talking with each other,

and in the moment before wind
kicks up between us, before it scatters litter
and teases their hair which they tuck away,

I see them. I see they are themselves
without regret. They're waving—
they want me to hurry.

Whatever emotion this is
must be over before I reach the car.

Violence

Joe McDonell rolled by us and the game changed. We'd
been cheering, whooping—we believed in teams—House,
Koenig, Carter, the others, all running, hitting someone,
getting hit, getting winded, hitting someone, first down after
first down, until we scored and went ahead and went crazy.
So we paid only half attention to the extra point, as Joe
McDonnell's leg swung back, paused, swung forward,
blocked, snapped like a broom stick, and he was buried in
the pile up. Even from their knees, players motioned. What
they heard must have scared them.

I worked that summer as a stacker in a box mill. 1967.
Ammo crates, berry flats a week in July, more ammo
crates. We knew where they were going, but you have to
understand we'd punch in and the saws would run straight
through 8 to 4:30, fresh wood coming at you down oiled
steel, that steady roar something you heard only when you
left it: shut a door on it, wash your hands with pumice
soap, splash water on your face, then go back into it. July
and August four guys lost fingers, parts of fingers: hand in
a red towel—four weeks off and cash, so much a knuckle.
The saws stayed on, whining—that cathedral room sweet
with blood and fir-sap and sweat and then pine.

Three operations, ten months, and Joe McDonnell walked
without crutches. He graduated with the rest of us. We left
home—college or the draft—the mill closed, the war ended.
I don't understand why or how this comes back from wood
smell or football on the radio. You're driving to pick up your
daughter—it's there. You're not in it, just watching. You
know what will happen, the next thing and the next. Like
turning a corner, a girl in the distance waiting just where
she said she'd be.

Fans

They gather around their coach,
score at the half 2-18. We stand, stretch,
joke about the platitudes we shall recite
into the car's silence on the way home:
they shot well, they were taller,
it wasn't your day, it's only a game.

All February and half of March we have practiced
active disinterest, our wishes for our children
always hopeless and the same. Last week
though they did not win, they did not quit.
This week, now, suddenly the trap works,
lay-ups fall. As the third quarter ends

they are winded, purposeful—they have tied the score.
Clenching hands and talking, nodding earnestly, they
know, even as they break and run for the drinking
fountain, even as they catch their breath, sit down, listen
to their coach, try to rest, they know
they will win. Watching them, we know how rare

are the chances to start over even. So we grin
as play resumes and they score. We high-five, holler
until we're hoarse. We can't believe we're here.
Our team hits 26 points to the other side's sad 2.
28-20. The clock counts down, we're on our feet
whooping, shouting, congratulating every winner,

my daughter the one who hugs me fiercely, tightly,
then runs after her teammates who are holy-jumping-up-
and-down-Martha thirteen years old, young women, hands
over their heads, sweaty, red-faced screaming at each
other, at this unlikely moment they have made together
and probably won't remember.

Arrowood House

Proud, taunting, a neighbor girl on wobbly wheels
has ridden by, and you have seen her. Right now
you will learn to ride a bicycle. You say so.

You roll the two wheeler to a flat, quiet street.
When you climb on and sit, the toes of your shoes
almost touch—you lean one side or the other.

I hold upright the back of the seat. "Ready?"
I start a slow jog. All your weight leans away
and I half stop the fall, and half not.

If you are hurt, you will not say. I apologize.
We try again. Running along, I can tell
what needs to click in the center of balance

is for you now only envy, will, a trust
in mystery, in what you cannot find. We try
again, again, again, until you're fighting tears.

I can no more do this for you than fly. I forget
how many days it took, how many times
falling was the price and the end. I remember

an evening after dinner. The bicycle,
as I run, as you peddle, floats free: you know,
and I let go. You have done this for yourself.

I am unsure how to turn or stop.
I see you balanced, upright,
one of the world's happiest children.

Brigadoon at the High School

An evening lost, though pleasantly—
that's it, all you figure on.
Then you walk in, breathe that nervous air
and God forbid you're fourteen, gawky,
healthy as a horse. No clothing
exactly fits. Hair wrong, face blotchy,
you probably look horrible, so shy you're mute
or garrulous, false as a senator.
And when the house lights dim
and rise on *Our Town* or this time *Brigadoon,*
what you see under the actors' veneer is terror—
the resolve of more than usual hope,
hope in rehearsal, in mindless repetition,
in sets and props and other actors
just as hopeful. You notice
how because it's not professional, that first
kiss makes the audience gasp. Fiona and Tommy
aren't playing at this because they don't know
how to yet, don't know how to not feel it,
which is their gracious, awkward gift
to themselves, to us—this public chance
to kiss another human being who may just be
beautiful. Ragged or smooth as this performance is
with set changes, a lengthy intermission, something
unplanned and vaguely ridiculous happens—
something you recognize comes back
in bright faces and sings.

Overlook House

"See, they return, and bring us with them."
                                                          T.S. Eliot

Wind the ocean of air eases in lazy arcs
all S's past windows cranked open on June's last day.
Douglas firs raise up their black arms.
The drilled and the wind-seeded
tassel and berry on tall blonde stalks.
And since presumably now they know,

I would like to ask two women, deceased, only memory,
where we come from, nematode and flat worm,
the deep ocean vents, their sulfurous ecosystems,
and to what in what dimension we proceed.
I would like to interrogate the electrons
of this valley, neither at rest nor in motion,

grain elevator, steel rolling mill, tin-
roofed barns and the hourly bells, upright
poplars, tansy, and the roadside's petroleum
dust. I would like to grasp simple as stone
or cloud what matter is, energy, the formula
only another more intricate naming.

I'd like to hear this as easily as one daughter
in Corvallis, the other, for the moment phoning
from Rome, and their mother working the schedules in Salem.
I would like to hear this because whatever it is
recurs like the lesson day and night, blossom
and fruit, endlessly, so far—

out of reach, insistent, but quiet.

Anniversary Again

His eyes are closed.
But the intelligence of his fingertips
       leads them to her skin
asleep in the morning.
       He traces her temple, the soft indent there,
warm where blood pulses. He finds the line
       where hairs thicken and sweep back
(his fingers know the texture there by heart),
       eyebrow and forehead and hers.
She sleeps and sleeps, an even breathing
       in the lightless hour
before dawn, before intention or mistake,
       nothing unsaid or heard or said.
He believes in fingers, touch,
       life of the skin, life of the body.
He believes in privilege,
       this proximity granted by promise,
believes unthinking touch, simple tenderness,
       graces all it touches, ageless
and incorruptible in the sleeping world.
       He reaches to touch her face, or she
to touch his, or he to touch his,
       or she to touch hers—the human motion.
Thirty years for us September 11, 2001.

Lost Inventory

Mornings and mornings rain closed the windows.
Morning the power slept and nothing woke us.
Morning a piano sounded up through the floor,
notes stuttering into melody, flaring away.

Morning the quail paraded their topknots
nodding over the white-painted margins of their faces.
Morning the swallows arrived, morning
the elevator froze. That sunlight

on the morning tiles, the phone unrung.
Mornings cumulus scoured the blue clean.
August morning the deer bedded under the maple.
Morning you turned half-dressed to me,

something you were about to say.
Morning I could not rise. Morning
before that morning, before that morning.
Nights the Perseids, utterly silent, lined by.

Limp nights that flattened us.
Nights coyotes woke the dogs. The night
she was born. And that night before she was born—
still, dreamless,

snow over everything.

Letter to Our Daughters

Rain today, then sun, then hail
       enough to whiten fields plowed for wheat.
For an hour I dug the row of raspberry canes—roots
       so exuberant they tunnel in every direction,
and the wintered-over great thistles of artichoke
       want to bloom and bloom. Lately
       we've restricted our intake of news, the worst places,
where children live with gunshot walls,
tanks in the streets, orchards trashed and wires down.
       Their faces have names in languages I don't know.
Parents gone, they share with their grandmother
       and wish they could go to school.
Do they also wish to kill what or who has done this?
       I fear the stories of their childhoods, if they will live
       to tell them or want to. Just the refrigerator humming
can seem obscene. News does this—
always war somewhere. It filters in.
       The two tomato plants on the porch
I will tomorrow release from their black plastic
       and set in the ground; with luck, they should be
bearing, as should the raspberries, if you visit in August.
       May no troops and no fear order your streets
emptied at dusk. May you sleep unoccupied,
       always without gunfire or dreams of it.
May safe water flow. Last evening as I sat in this chair,
       a skunk, tail low, walked its odd gait away.
Earlier, a doe, stately, grand and deeply pregnant,
       slowly traversed the gravel. Allergies soon,
such is May. Sorry for the long digression.
       No one of us who chooses can be perfect.
We think of you every day, and I write to think of you,
       and not often enough.

Immersion

Water so recently Arctic,
    That first surprise stays unsayable, onshore
Then pulling at your eroding heels.
    An ache like death rises and you dance
Foolishly—howl or moan
    As the foamed, prismatic surface
Climbs your shins, your knees,
    As you go on stubbornly west, downhill,
Waves taller than you are,
Impacts like huge open hands.

Held in that tidal constricting cold,
    Breathe, breathe little breaths, because blood
Does get used to where you are,
    Which is deeper, perverse with surf perch
And Dungeness, that first metallic panic
    Saying you're crazy doing this, though the current
Seems warmer, and chest-high swells
    Lift you, and the largest breakers rise and curve,
Lucent green brightest at their thinnest,
    The heart you close your eyes and dive for
Into silence and shock, going nowhere.
    The wave breaking over rattles down
The chakras of your spine. You tumble,
    Shoved rudely to sand, pressure, absence of air,
A dark floor you palm and push from.
    Then your face surfaces
In air lovely before speech,
Summer, the new world.

Deep Summer, Nothing to Say

Ripe yellow corn, husks shucked
and blonde silks pulled, boiled, buttered,
        taken four rows, and four more
and more—our sloppy sweet meal done,
        twilight's pale crimson blue to grape
rises in the east, shadows not gone half
        an hour, wheat straw blanched
under the Appenines of the moon.

Of this our inheritance—surface of earth
        heaved, sunk, gouged, fired, swept;
of rock and dust, accident, urge, anger's
        bile and bloody words; and once, a tourist,
Piazza Santa Croce, startled, then held
        in Dante's scowl and marble gaze—who
is not unconscious and unworthy?

Warm dusk. No chore. A decent chair.
        Blank rhythm, mute rhyme: light
does what light does, on planetary time.

The Waiting

Late bees convene, they interrogate the porch.
Paper wasps held together by god knows what
visit the seat-sprung, the cane back chairs.
Dark snow goes uphill in narrower runnels
on mountains hazed into distance.
Tired summer hangs on.

We are not met.
The hand we seek, the one in dreams
that laves our faces and hums the unremembered song—
the hand, the gesture and all its benevolence
darkens nothing, offers nothing.

If we knew for certain what was needed.
If we knew precisely the process, step-by-step,
rules for the dance, orders for the colors
of one bougainvillaea, lilac, or Norway maple.
If we knew why they sing in our eyes.
If we could say the name, the perfect sounds
for ground we love. That, and the common litany—
how this becomes this becomes mango
and bird of paradise, cocoa bean, skunk cabbage.
If we could say why.
If we could know the title of any rainwater, river, well
water, the miles and endless minutes
in the clear glass we drink from. If
we could rouse and tease the dead
or ourselves unborn.
But we are not met.

The harrowed fields are so carefully groomed
they've become sculpture, all parallels and contours.
Blackberries fatten. The long shadows of 6:20pm
stretch out and recline under an unstarred blue.
The light goes rose, golden. We talk.

III.

One Time

(Airport Beach, Maui)

When they use those masks and snorkels,

when they wade through shorebreak into the blue green
and stand on the coarse-grain rippled bottom,

when they float out on a northwest swell, scull and turn
down to silence and old lava rich with corals,

they will discover the orange spine unicorn fish,
its tail attached by a pink bow,

its face like a mandrill. They will discover
yellow tangs, the black-then-yellow butterfly fish,

eye-stripe surgeonfish, a dozen goat fish
hanging like sleepers in the surge and ebb,

and the triggerfish with blue neon lips it puckers
when it puffs from its mouth and exhales from its gills

whatever from the reef bottom it cannot eat.
Older by four days in this place,

I know they cannot believe the altitude or distance
of their journey here, unfamiliar hours, air

and water the temperature of skin. Early morning
the trades are a soft breathing off Molokai.

They want a picture, the one time I will ever see them,
my pleasure: *one, two,* and the shutter open on *three.*

Forest Service Survey at Cold Water Springs

Backs sore, calves sore, eyes pinched,
we have walked dusty, piney ground
for what we want to imagine—the past in glassy flakes
wherever it might have fallen in toolmaking
by this springs, snowmelt welling out of rocky dirt,
hurrying then persuasively through the grass. Noon,
so we stop, walk a path marked with pin flags, each
a random, smoky shard. We walk down
to do what people do on a hot dry day in June
in the moon of making fat—same water,
same path, same thirst.

No one that morning found a spear point
or an arrow point or scraper resting
where something set down might stay
storms, seasons, afternoons and cool evenings
untouched in the air, while the hand that set it down
forgot and moved on, maybe to cup that cold water
or shelter with children at the overhang
under the natural chimney, near the fire
while rain fell or snow.

Only a little wind west rattled the aspens.
The water did not so much pressure up as simply
appear, invisible except for the sun's catching it
and how it swayed grasses. By afternoon
we'd learned to angle the light, settle on our heels
and wait for whatever might glint in all that dust
and duff, needles longer than fingers.

We learned a warm and pleasant languor:
what's sought will appear sooner or late, or not,
attention the reason, afternoon, sage smell,
lava rock, life of the body
and the one earth.

Beach Agates

Wherever they were
with kelp leaves or the worn smooth
centers of clams, or scattered
with mussels' blue neon interiors,
sea sponge and the shredded coral,

as water foamed and advanced
and gulls beat low into wind,
these waited until we found them
amber or paler yellow, quartz white
among red jasper, the blues

black in the shade. They are liquid
hardened, seamed, flawed, occluded.
They push memory such distances
imagining them humbles anyone.
Look up: all is green and silver—

the heavy surface of the sea.
But these are light, each
a particular light and smooth persistence—
they ought to testify.
They ought to say something

beyond tidal order, random currents.
They are the origin and dream of glass.
Whatever they say is impersonal.
Whatever it is is beautiful.

Kirsteen Burton

Beyond the double vowels and cadence of her name,
you don't know her, nor do I. I know a plaque on a bench.
I pass it when I run in the park.

All the dark winter of rain, no one sits there.
By April a chilly parent watches children on tricycles.
In July an elderly person rests with a panting schnauzer.

In the hazy August of Queen Anne's lace, I notice
velvet red wedged in the slats near the bronze rectangle,
near the engraving. A mile later

I've looped back, dripping, winded.
The park's empty. I stop, read what's there:
the name we know, two dates: she died in her 20's.

And someone who paid for that bench and this privilege
on this one particular day bought two roses
or cut them from a garden, gorgeous Mr. Lincolns,

brought them, sat here feeling something
whatever it was, whatever it was like, sat back to her name
on her bench and looked out at new houses, a natural field.

Then stood, slid the green spines between the slats,
looked at them and walked away, which is all you can do.
As though we thought we were not all forgotten.

The Moon

"Nothing changes, moon of my delight."
Leopardi

In afternoons in June
it rests in the blue, the reliable firmament,
and makes no response. If green swallows dip
and loop on some errand known only to them, if
traffic backs up and horns blare, tempers vocal
and near to violence, if in some dark
bar the drinker who started at 11
topples from the stool and the bartender says
"shit," and does nothing else, if someone napping
wakes and chooses to say nothing, chooses
to turn away, if rain rattles the cottonwoods
then drips for an hour after the downpour, if hurt
arrives with its cheery cousins impotence and desire
and clothes don't fit, milk sour, no
cash in the wallet, the tank sugared, tires slashed
or just too weary to hold under pressure, if clouds
obscure the moon, it doesn't care.
It rests. It rests in the blue,
the reliable firmament.
Even half gone in afternoons in June,
it abides there and it doesn't care.
It abides there and doesn't care.

No Levitation, No Song

Nine years old,
    he has learned to smoke.
His older brother taught him.

    And ten years old,
he teaches his brother, thirteen,
how Scotch scorches a throat,

how stolen cut beer
runs through kidneys like water
    through a headgate.

    Their father dies—
a stomach full of cancer,
his hair at forty-eight

the color of high cirrus in August,
    that month his mother took to bed
and never quite roused

even as she washed neighbors' shirts,
starched and ironed their collars
    and their cuffs.

His older brother loved a woman,
    age seventeen, as his way away.
Younger, responsible, he stayed

    with that washerwoman
in that house a dead father and husband
had built and left.

    Afternoons, she heated the irons.
One spring he acted in a play
in borrowed, buffed black shoes.

His brother wrote only checks,
        then stopped.
How his mother sickened slowly

sickened him,
        terror and anger
unrinsable tin in his mouth.

        He was happy she died.

Now, eighty-six, whole inches shorter,
knuckles of his fists like bulbs,
        he remembers the wife

        he so fully wanted to love,
does crosswords, cracks jokes.
His knees want to fail—

he won't let them. He is one watery-eyed
        unwilling old man,
terrified again if he ever wasn't,

soberer than he wants to be—
facts he'd no more admit
        than levitate or sing.

We look at each other
        across a table in July, where
it's true what they say—we are all free.

It takes both his hands
to lift iced tea in its wet glass
        and set it down.

He knows how to smoke
sixty years and quit.
      Knows by heart

      every seduction
of stuffed olives, vodka, gin,
and turns away.

      Knows how to earn
and cash a check, knows work,
which has so rudely left him,

and how to bury his dead.

Green

Lebanon to Hebo, Iron Mountain
to Mary's Peak, over the rumpled
sheet of this valley, color begins.
Rose of Nootka roses, white petals
of blackberries, mountain ash,
cadmium of Scotch broom on upslopes—
it makes the brown of dirt, the sillion
of plowed fields, browner, not flat
but fertile, the nativity of color.

And by late spring in this valley,
what the world wants in its visible way
to say before it goes torrid, limp and drought-weary,
the message I miss in distraction every year
is green. Green of marshes shrinking.
Green of duck feathers. The slick
sheen of the tops of cottonwood leaves
and the flat silver of their undersides,
their semaphore on and off in wind,
black and pewter in moonlight.

Yellow-green of willows, alders.
The sterner iron of oak leaves
and the pliable flags of maples, black
firs, their new tassels, the outsides
and the insides. New wheat or foxglove,
vanilla leaf, whatever it means,
grand fir or red cedar—whatever it means
is green, whatever it means.

Feet Up, Heads Down

Seamed now,
long cracked in its cooling, smooth
     as gravity, wide as a freeway—

this basalt rapped by a stick
     echoes not at all: no hollow, nothing.
It's its own thickness all the way down,

     all the way, our parents said, to China
where, as they see us, we stand feet up, heads down,
     our words babble, whatever holding us

a matter for physics which is magic.
     Tide scoured, unbarnacled, this flow
floors a sand cliff, a sheer, irregular tumble

     seeded by beach peas, sedges and rushes,
a small ecology present in its erosion.
     On a hundred-year dune, salal, lupine,

salmonberry, *pinus contorta*, new spruce
     wall a trail shoulder high—
thorns, needles, and throngs of white bells.

     They argue not geology but sex,
not density but translucence, season and bloom,
     pelican veer and return, oystercatchers

in silly boots. They argue the promise
     basalt ignores—promise of impermanence,
joy of goodbye and hello, promise of fruit.

     All day at the ebb and flood of tide,
we move among the elements, small as people,
     odder than birds, on a blue ball.

Monday, April 6th

The watercolor calendar says Albrecht Dürer
painted this alpine View of Arco while traveling
        from Nuremberg to Italy in 1495—
one of "the first landscapes ever in the history
        of Western watercolor." You can tell when
he traveled: late spring, deciduous trees
        entirely leafed out—green blurs,
elms maybe, beeches or oaks. You can tell
        he loved how the brown road disappears
into a grove or behind a wall, how it S curves out.
        You can tell how luxurious it was—and is—
to love everything in sight, all so nicely
        distanced individuals disappear
and what's clear is only their work on the land:
        a vineyard, several walled enclosures, a fortress
on a sheer hill rimmed with watch towers—
        tiny lines and rectangles and deft shading
all claiming order, long history,
        labor, society, safety. Oddly enough,
one of the natural formations of the hill looks
        like the face of someone either angry or about
to sneeze. Dürer must have seen this
        if I can, whatever it means. I think
it means he had a sense of humor. What I
        envy is the time, several good-
weather days and enough food, enough
        amplitude of schedule to linger—maybe
animals were lame—to paint this watercolor,
        just because he was there and might not
be back, because that view, its shapes
        and shadings, appealed to his eye and the paints
were handy, a clutch of brushes, an $8^3/4$ inch
        square of paper, and it was something he could do—
put it all down flat and deceptive
        under his live signature.

Wasp

Warily, rolled magazine in hand,
I am watching a death on Halloween,
a fat wasp called by my open window's warm

and siren promise: all winter sweet repose
waking into April. In this it joins box elder bugs,
spiders, the garage's dense clutch of ladybugs—

everything wants in. Earth's mosaic—
soil of nematodes, shining surface of slugs,
water of ouzels, air of gnats—

everything wants to prolong itself.
So the wasp circles.
Investigates the slats of Venetian blinds,

the narrow canyons between upright books.
It cannot understand my lemon ginger tea.
If I look hard enough I imagine seeing

the actual motion of its blurred wings.
I no longer have the heart to swat at it.
What sound do red leaves flaming make,

the brown leaves unfallen?
Welcome all.
More than one clock ticks.

Day Litany

Buffed chrome. Velour
on the couch, the solid ketchup stain.
Heron and harbor seals,
quartersawn oak, gerbera daisies, celluloid
and hair color, cotton fibers, white
violets, coffee and the Sphinx face.

Dodo, piano notes, Gibson guitar.
Dandelion bloom, dandelion tap root. Rose
glass, verdigris, calico and gargoyle, and fan
belts, capped teeth, silk ties, the engine
at HO scale. Barbie doll, clam
chowder, the soft white

incandescents. Crystal
radio, hand grenade and cat's eye
marbles, steam from a kettle, oolong
and scars from stitches, notes
in the air, intention in the ear, chair-
backs, spumoni, a pleated shade.

Hail stones, sling shot and wheat grass,
mole hill and mole, marsupial and chondrite,
electricity and the oxygen of fire,
chocolate, or history with all its attachments,
and granite and baby's breath, wherever
it comes from and wherever it goes.

Pink

Firs with their upswept skirts,
cottonwoods shedding, yellowed
and not quite vertical in the early light,
maples like deep bowls,
and cedars, dark triangles at the pasture corners,
the pasture flooded with ground mist, white
dew, bleached angora layered in the distance. . .

Nothing's happened yet.
Though the pitted road is clogged, clotted with cars,
though in many bathrooms showers deliver downpours,
though coffee filters and drips, toast
toasts and the tea steeps.

I haven't said a word yet to anyone
nor heard anything but the junco, the chickadee,
sister crow calling her numerous cousins
in the steadily diminishing oaks,
each leaf a piece of the ghost
they're giving up, each
a little plaything,
a pebble for the wind to scuff.

It's a good time,
sun a pink brush stroke and steady rumor,
hawks half-sleeping in branches by the highway.
It's a good time. Heat ducts pop in their joints,
the body's ecology
all rhythm and back-stretching
back in the world of touch.

Morning Walk with Gerard Manley Hopkins

Nothing is so beautiful as Spring
       which has taken us to this, August
and its hot breath. . .
Hillsides exhale,
       brown, hard as platters.
Wild carrot, Queen Anne's lace,
each saucer draining its reservoir.

*

Thrush's eggs look little low heavens
       and the fledged birds gorge.
Fat as arms, gopher snakes
tattoo and burrow deeper.
       By thin water, killdeer linger,
oaks going metallic, shutting down.
A ground squirrel in a silver vest
       stands on its back legs,
sermon, credo, some warning or rebuke
I can't make a word of.

*

What is all this juice and all this joy?
       Swallows and turkey vultures,
tansy nodding in its yellow crowns,
under the white, hot sun.
       Berries on the tongue,
sweet tonic and seeds in the teeth. . .
I can do this for twenty minutes or so,
       an hour, I can do this, be lost,
unfound, under descending blue,
loose and thirsty in a body.

What Wind Says

Nothing. I am not searching. Little
dogs, the multiples of insect wings.
Diesel, sulfur, ozone and stew, searing
oxides, the poisonous wishes. Mice at rest.
Four days and half-moony, nimbus nights,
apple blossoms. Two days past hard frost,
the slumping pumpkins. Sailcloth, silos, tee
shirts, white sleeves. Air, ocean, skunk
cabbage, bog. Conscious gutturals, nasals,
—animals odd as sloths and giraffes, hippos
and dingoes eating or greeting. Pollen, weepy
eyes. Pressures old as Jupiter. Swallows
and vultures, vowels at Aeolian windows.
Reverb over bottles, *sh* over ears.

My Week of Silence

First, brand names fell away.
They sifted into corners and unlike dust became
        what they were before: inks returned to soy,
cardboard become the tongue and groove of a floor,
        become the tree, the flower, the pollen,
winter rain, cloud, ocean, and so on.

        Too easy greetings
had to be stifled; they became
        friendliness about the mouth, a nod,
or, if inclined, a ceremonial bow
        as you reached for the brown-sugar bowl
and found another hand there before yours.

        Eating, you hear your own teeth
grinding what lived elsewhere and on its own—
        the texture, taste, and water you swallow.
When was the bell announcing the hour?
        Voices forgotten come to you
because you say nothing to stop them.

        The child you were knocks on your door.
Then your awkwardnesses and broken pieces
        organize a game of Simon Says on the lawn
as you watch from the quiet porch.
        Rain and skin require no translation.
Nations are the actions of people.

You cannot save the dog from the car.

The Vegetable Vendor

Dust thick on the plank floor,
Walls unpainted lath and plaster,
Echoing up from somewhere and repeating
In one of memory's first, oldest rooms—
Hooves on pavement, iron shoes
In a four-part rhythm growing louder.

A wooden-wheeled wagon, tin scales
Like justice, ash spokes in a rim inset with iron
Pitted and almost black, cold to touch.
In crates packed with dripping ice, wet cabbage rounds
Nestle tooth and jowl, artichokes tight-fisted
Over their purple explosions, rhubarb in ruby stalks,
Buffed eggplant, cauliflower brains, and the unopened
Flowerlets of broccoli.

I can see the hocks of legs—horse or mule,
A steady drip from the darkened slats,
Leather shoes not mine, cuffed pants.
I hear words in an accent I can't repeat.
The driveway's downhill bands of concrete to the street.
Irvington, any season but winter, 19 and 54,
So many people I read or love or admire later
Separate in their lives—children or older.
I manage one huge lettuce head to the door.

Letter to Ourselves from Placid

Cracked, useless as an old Timex,
the Nikon rests at home in its parts
in the drawer with nuts, lock washers,
unmatchable bolts. Travel assumes
the unreality of history, and the sun
fills us with languorous desire. Therefore,
we imagine paper, a letter to ourselves
returned amid extraordinary laundry.

Here, out there, mergansers:
their neon crowns are sexual displays.
Placid Lake fills a bowl a blue mile
half full, sides bristly with larch a green
entirely their own. To imagine the cabin
say *cabin, screendoor.* A propane icebox
hums its cargo of beer. Here is here,
and we are not opening envelopes.

No news arrives. We have no pictures.
Earlier, we swam. Later we threw rocks
for the splashes. Cattle blur on the far shore.
We have used all our fingers to count deer.
Two of them cool their withers in lake water.
Bats roost under the back porch roof.
Today we are going nowhere. We can tell
each other almost anything.

Born and raised in Portland, Lex Runciman has lived most of his life in Oregon's Willamette Valley. Along the way, he has worked as a warehouseman, shipping-receiving clerk, and a stacker in a box mill. He is the author of two earlier books of poems: *Luck* (1981) and *The Admirations* (1989), which won the Oregon Book Award. He holds graduate degrees from the writing programs at the University of Montana and the University of Utah. A co-editor of two anthologies, *Northwest Variety: Personal Essays by 14 Regional Authors* and *Where We Are: The Montana Poets Anthology,* his own work has appeared in several anthologies including, *From Here We Speak, Portland Lights* and *O Poetry, O Poesia.* He was adopted at birth. He and Deborah Jane Berry Runciman have been married thirty-two years and are the parents of two grown daughters. He taught for eleven years at Oregon State University and is now Professor of English at Linfield College, where he received the Edith Green Award in teaching in 1997.